Introduction to the Philosophy of Socrates

Zack Horton

© 2015 Logos Publishing

All rights reserved. No part of this publication may be reproduced, distributed, or transmitted in any form or by any means, including photocopying, recording, or other electronic or mechanical methods, without the prior written permission of the publisher, except in the case of brief quotations embodied in critical reviews and certain other noncommercial uses permitted by copyright law.

Table of Contents

Introduction 7
Chapter 1: The Life of Socrates 10
   1.1 Early Life and Upbringing 10
   1.2 Socratic Turn: Shift to Philosophy 12
   1.3 Socrates in Athens: Daily Life and Personality 13
   1.4 Trial and Death of Socrates 16
Chapter 2: Socratic Philosophy 18
   2.1 Defining the Socratic Method 18
   2.2 Socratic Irony 21
   2.3 Elenchus: The Art of Refutation .. 23
   2.4 Criticisms and Implications 25
Chapter 3: Socratic Paradoxes 28
   3.1 Defining Socratic Paradoxes 28
   3.2 Nobody Does Wrong Knowingly. 30
   3.3 Virtue is Knowledge 31
   3.4 Virtue is the Highest Form of Good 33
Chapter 4: Socrates and Politics 36

4.1 Political Stance and Athenian Politics 36

4.2 Critique of Democracy 38

4.3 Impact on Athenian Democracy ... 40

4.4 Trial and Execution: A Democratic Verdict 42

Chapter 5: Socrates and His Influence ... 45

5.1 Socrates and Plato: Profound Influence 45

5.2 The Platonic Socrates 48

5.3 Xenophon's Recollection 49

5.4 Differences Between Xenophon and Plato's Accounts 51

Chapter 6: Socrates and Religion 54

6.1 Socrates' Views on Religion 54

6.2 Charges of Impiety 57

6.3 The "Divine Sign" 59

6.4 Impact on Greek Religious Thought 60

Chapter 7: The Ethics of Socrates 63

7.1 Socratic Ethics Defined 63

7.2 The Role of Reason in Ethics 65

7.3 Virtue Ethics 68

7.4 The Socratic Conception of Happiness 70

Chapter 8: Socrates in Subsequent Philosophical Thought 72

8.1 Socrates in Hellenistic Philosophy 72

8.2 Socrates in Medieval Philosophy .. 75

8.3 Socrates in Modern and Contemporary Philosophy 78

8.4 The Global Reception of Socratic Thought 81

Chapter 9: Socrates in Art, Literature, and Popular Culture 84

9.1 Socrates in Ancient Art 84

9.2 Socrates in Literature 87

9.3 Socrates in Modern Art, Film, and Television 89

9.4 The Popular Image of Socrates 91

Chapter 10: Evaluating Socrates: Historical and Philosophical Assessment 94

10.1 Historical Assessment 94

10.2 Influence on Western Philosophy 96

10.3 Socrates in Education 98
10.4 Relevance of Socratic Philosophy Today.. 100
Glossary 103
Further Reading.. 111

Introduction

The name Socrates has been synonymous with wisdom, philosophy, and critical thought for more than two millennia. Born in the late 5th century BCE in Athens, Socrates never penned a single line of text. Yet, his influence permeates the very fabric of Western philosophy, reaching far beyond the realm of academia and into popular consciousness. Despite—or perhaps due to—the inherent complexities surrounding the study of a figure who left no writings of his own, Socrates remains a source of endless fascination and inquiry. This book, titled simply "Socrates", is an exploration of the man, his philosophy, and his enduring legacy.

Socrates lived and philosophized at a time when Athens was a vibrant center of art, science, and political thought. Yet his life, as chronicled by his disciples Plato and Xenophon and satirized by the playwright Aristophanes, stood out for its singular devotion to the pursuit of wisdom. From his role as a stonemason in his early years to his unwavering commitment to philosophy and his eventual trial and execution, Socrates' life story forms the foundation upon which his philosophical contributions rest. To understand Socrates' philosophy is, in part, to understand his life.

The philosophy of Socrates is characterized by a distinctive approach, a unique method of inquiry now known as the Socratic Method, or elenchus. By relentless questioning and refutation of false beliefs, Socrates sought to stimulate critical thinking, fostering a profound shift in the way knowledge and understanding were pursued in the ancient world. This book aims to illuminate the intricacies of this method and the far-reaching implications it has had for the philosophical tradition.

Integral to Socratic thought are his paradoxes and ethical ideas—his belief that "virtue is knowledge," his argument that "no one does wrong knowingly," and his view that virtue is the highest form of good. Each of these seemingly contradictory yet deeply insightful propositions offers a unique lens to view Socratic philosophy. Understanding these principles is essential to grasp the depth and scope of Socratic ethics, which placed an unparalleled emphasis on virtue and the good life.

Socrates' impact on Western philosophy is vast and enduring, but his influence extends beyond philosophy. His thoughts on politics, religion, and education have left a mark on these fields, prompting reevaluations, adaptations, and sometimes, controversies. This book delves into these areas, shedding light on Socrates' views and the ways in which they have shaped—and continue to shape—societal structures and norms.

As a figure who has been embraced, debated, and reinterpreted throughout history, Socrates continues to inspire a diverse range of reactions. From the veneration of his followers and the condemnation of his detractors to his depiction in art and literature, the reception of Socrates is as complex as the philosopher himself. A careful exploration of these receptions is essential for a well-rounded understanding of Socrates' role and significance in history.

Chapter 1: The Life of Socrates

1.1 Early Life and Upbringing

Socrates was born in the city of Athens in 469 BC, a time when the ancient city-state was rising to the peak of its political and cultural influence. The precise details of his birth are relatively unknown, largely due to the lack of contemporary sources focused on his early life.

The son of Sophroniscus, a stonemason, and Phaenarete, a midwife, Socrates belonged to the middle socio-economic class of Athenian society, termed the zeugitai. Although not from an aristocratic background, he was able to receive a basic education which likely included reading, writing, music, and gymnastics, as was common for Athenian males of the time.

As a young man, it is believed that Socrates initially followed his father's profession, given a reference to his "work in stone" found in Plato's dialogue, the Symposium (Plato, 200e–201c)3. This profession could have provided Socrates with a pragmatic and hands-on perspective on life, which later found expression in his philosophical approach.

Socrates served as a hoplite, or heavily armed infantryman, in the Athenian military during several campaigns. Notable among these were the Siege of Potidaea (432–429 BC), the Battle of Delium (424 BC), and the Battle of Amphipolis (422 BC). His courage and resilience during these campaigns are well-documented in the accounts of both Plato and Xenophon.

Socrates' early life was marked by a unique blend of common Athenian upbringing and his personal journey in a milieu of burgeoning intellectual curiosity. The Athens of his time was a hub of philosophical, political, and cultural innovation, all of which would have significantly shaped the young philosopher's mind and left an indelible mark on his life's work.

1.2 Socratic Turn: Shift to Philosophy

The precise moment when Socrates turned towards philosophy, dubbed as the 'Socratic Turn', is difficult to pinpoint due to a scarcity of direct historical evidence. However, Plato's dialogues provide us with some clues.

In the dialogue "Phaedrus," Socrates spoke of his preference for the learning derived from direct human interaction over knowledge gathered from books, suggesting an early tendency towards introspective philosophical inquiry.

One significant event that could mark the Socratic turn was his encounter with the Oracle of Delphi. According to Plato's "Apology," the Pythia, the priestess of the Delphic Oracle, proclaimed that no one was wiser than Socrates. This pronouncement perplexed Socrates, as he was aware of his own ignorance. He embarked on a journey to interpret the oracle's meaning, questioning those reputed to be wise in Athenian society. This began his method of elenchus, or refutation, challenging those who believed they possessed wisdom, revealing their lack of true understanding, and his own wisdom in recognizing his ignorance.

Socrates spent much of his later life in the marketplace and public places of Athens, engaging in dialogue with anyone willing to converse, regardless of their social standing. These included wealthy aristocrats, politicians, poets, craftsmen, and even slaves. His philosophical approach, later termed the "Socratic Method," involved asking probing questions to reveal contradictions in the beliefs of his interlocutors, ultimately aiming at achieving clearer understanding and insight.

Socrates' shift towards philosophy wasn't a transition from one profession to another in the conventional sense. Rather, it was an inner reorientation, a commitment to a certain way of life which he pursued not as a paid teacher, but as a citizen philosopher devoted to the pursuit of ethical understanding and wisdom.

1.3 Socrates in Athens: Daily Life and Personality

Socrates was a highly visible figure in the city of Athens. His daily routine largely consisted of public discourse. He spent much of his time in the marketplace, the Agora, conversing with those around him, asking questions and stimulating debate. He seemed to take delight in the bustling public life of Athens, readily engaging in philosophical discourse with anyone interested in conversation, irrespective of their social class or professional background.

Socrates lived a life of austere simplicity, seemingly indifferent to material comforts. He was often barefoot and wore the same cloak in both winter and summe. His ascetic lifestyle, however, did not prevent him from enjoying the conviviality of feasts, as depicted in Plato's "Symposium" and Xenophon's "Symposium" where he is a central figure at the drinking parties.

His personality, as portrayed by his disciples, was characterized by an unwavering commitment to philosophical inquiry and ethical integrity. He was described as having an enduring physical and mental endurance, a sharp wit, and a deep sense of irony. This distinctive combination of attributes played a crucial role in shaping the Socratic method of dialogue and inquiry.

Socrates was known to be guided by what he called his 'daimonion' or 'divine sign,' an inner voice that did not instruct him on what to do but prevented him from doing certain things. He referred to this spiritual guidance in his defense during his trial, claiming it as a gift from the gods.

Despite his popularity, Socrates was a controversial figure. His relentless questioning often embarrassed those who considered themselves wise, leading to resentment and ultimately contributing to his trial and execution.

Socrates' life in Athens was marked by his steadfast devotion to philosophy and his tireless pursuit of wisdom. His daily routine, personality, and values were deeply entwined with his philosophical endeavors, contributing significantly to his legacy and impact on Western philosophy.

1.4 Trial and Death of Socrates

In 399 BC, Socrates was brought to trial on charges of impiety and corrupting the youth of Athens. The charge of impiety included not recognizing the gods acknowledged by the city and introducing new divine entities, presumably referring to his claim of guidance from his 'daimonion'. The charge of corrupting the youth was likely due to his influence on young Athenians, some of whom later became involved in political scandals, including the oligarchic coup of the Thirty Tyrants.

The trial took place in the People's Court of Athens, composed of a large jury of 500 male citizens selected by lot. Socrates was found guilty by a relatively close vote. After the conviction, Socrates was asked to propose a counter-penalty to the prosecution's suggestion of death. In an act of characteristic defiance and irony, Socrates first suggested he should be rewarded with free meals in the Prytaneum, a privilege granted to Athens' greatest benefactors. After the laughter subsided, he proposed a fine, which was rejected by the jury. The sentence was death by drinking a potion containing poison hemlock.

Between the sentencing and his execution, Socrates was held in an Athens prison. During this time, his followers, including Crito, proposed escape plans, but Socrates refused, arguing that a true philosopher should not fear death and that escaping would be breaking the laws he had always respected.

Socrates' final moments were spent in philosophical discourse with his friends on the immortality of the soul, as depicted in Plato's "Phaedo." According to the account, Socrates drank the hemlock with calm acceptance and died surrounded by his friends.

The trial and execution of Socrates, one of the most tragic episodes in the history of philosophy, are understood as a clash between an uncompromising individual and the democratic society that misunderstood his intent and teachings. His death marked the end of his life but the beginning of his immense philosophical legacy.

Chapter 2: Socratic Philosophy

2.1 Defining the Socratic Method

The Socratic Method, also known as Socratic questioning or elenchus, is a form of inquiry used to stimulate critical thinking and illuminate ideas. It involves a cooperative argumentative dialogue between individuals, based on asking and answering questions to stimulate critical thinking and draw out ideas and underlying presuppositions.

Socratic questioning is not teaching per se, but rather a method of inquiry and discussion between individuals, with the aim of seeking deeper understanding. Socratic dialogue is characterized by a demand for definitions, probing examples, seeking of implications and consequences, and refutations of inconsistencies in the interlocutor's responses.

Central to the Socratic Method is the

acknowledgment of one's own ignorance. Socrates often claimed that he knew nothing, which was not an assertion of absolute ignorance but an acknowledgment that he had no definitive knowledge of the virtues, which he was always seeking to understand.

In a typical Socratic dialogue, as illustrated in Plato's early dialogues, Socrates starts by questioning his interlocutor on a belief they hold, seeking a definition. When an answer is offered, Socrates questions it and points out its contradictions and inadequacies, leading the interlocutor to revise the answer or offer another. This process is repeated, often without arriving at a conclusive definition or understanding, resulting in what is called aporia, a state of puzzlement (Brickhouse and Smith, 2010)3.

It's important to note that the Socratic Method aims not at winning an argument, but at seeking wisdom and moral insight. By revealing our lack of knowledge, Socratic questioning encourages us to pursue a clearer, more humble understanding of the world around us.

The Socratic Method, while appearing simple on the surface, requires a deep commitment to critical thinking, self-assessment, and intellectual humility. Its relevance extends beyond philosophy, influencing areas such as teaching, psychotherapy, and legal practice.

2.2 Socratic Irony

Socratic irony is a technique employed by Socrates that involves feigning ignorance or modesty to expose the ignorance or contradictions in the argument of his interlocutor. The word "irony" derives from the Greek "eironeia," meaning "dissimulation," and Socrates' use of irony serves to stimulate the dialectical process and promote self-reflection and critical thinking.

A primary example of Socratic irony is Socrates' oft-repeated claim of his own ignorance. He famously asserted, "I know that I know nothing," a statement that seems paradoxical given his role as a philosopher. Yet, this expression of humility was a strategic move designed to encourage his interlocutors to examine their own knowledge critically.

Another facet of Socratic irony lies in his manner of questioning. Socrates often presented himself as a learner, asking others to teach him and explain their views. By doing so, he positioned his interlocutors as the supposed experts, subtly challenging them to defend their positions while revealing the inconsistencies in their beliefs.

Socratic irony should not be understood as sarcasm or mockery, but rather as a philosophical tool aimed at promoting a deeper understanding of the issues under discussion. It is an instrument of dialectic, a method of investigating the truth by examining the opposition between different ideas. Through irony, Socrates invites others (and us, the readers) to engage in this dialectical process, leading to a more profound, often humbling, insight into our knowledge and beliefs.

Socratic irony, then, is a subtle yet powerful component of the Socratic method. It underscores the philosopher's commitment to the pursuit of wisdom through continuous questioning and the willingness to acknowledge the limitations of one's knowledge.

2.3 Elenchus: The Art of Refutation

The term elenchus refers to the Socratic method of questioning, specifically the practice of refuting an interlocutor's argument to reveal its inconsistencies. Derived from the Greek "elenchein," meaning "to examine," "to refute," or "to cross-examine," elenchus forms the core of the Socratic method of inquiry.

In a Socratic dialogue, Socrates begins by asking his interlocutor to state a belief or definition about a certain virtue or concept. He then proceeds to question the interlocutor with the aim of challenging their assertion, typically resulting in a demonstration of its inadequacy or inconsistency. The goal of elenchus is not to defeat or embarrass the other person, but rather to expose the limits of knowledge and encourage deeper understanding.

Elenchus is particularly effective in revealing false or unexamined beliefs. By pushing the interlocutor to clarify, support, or revise their views, Socrates encourages self-reflection and critical assessment. The end of a Socratic refutation often leads to aporia, a state of puzzlement or impasse, signaling the need for further inquiry and reflection.

One of the most distinctive aspects of elenchus is that it is a collaborative process. It is not a monologue or lecture, but rather a dialogue between Socrates and his interlocutor. This collaborative aspect is key to the philosophical investigation, as it invites active participation and intellectual engagement.

It's important to note that while Socratic elenchus often results in the refutation of the interlocutor's initial belief, it does not necessarily provide a definitive or positive answer to the question at hand. The value of elenchus, according to Socrates, lies not in arriving at conclusive knowledge, but in the process of self-examination and the pursuit of wisdom.

Through the practice of elenchus, Socrates illuminated the complexities of human knowledge and moral understanding, leaving a lasting legacy on the field of philosophy.

2.4 Criticisms and Implications

The philosophy and methods of Socrates have been both influential and controversial throughout the history of Western philosophy. Despite its significant contribution to critical thinking, the Socratic Method, including the practice of elenchus and Socratic irony, has faced various criticisms and sparked extensive debates.

One critique revolves around the seemingly inconclusive nature of Socratic dialogue. Many of Socrates' conversations end in aporia, a state of puzzlement where no definitive answer is reached. Critics argue that this lack of concrete resolution can be dissatisfying or frustrating. However, proponents counter that the value of Socratic dialogue lies not in reaching a definitive answer but in the process of rigorous examination and self-reflection.

Another criticism of the Socratic Method concerns the potential for manipulative discourse. Socrates often guides his interlocutors towards a realization of their own ignorance, which some interpret as a tactic of intellectual domination. However, others argue that this is a misinterpretation of Socrates' intent, which was to stimulate critical thinking and illuminate truths.

Despite these criticisms, the implications and influence of Socratic philosophy are profound. The Socratic Method has found application in various fields beyond philosophy, including law, education, and psychotherapy. It promotes critical thinking, encourages intellectual humility, and fosters a spirit of inquiry, making it a cornerstone of democratic discourse.

Socrates' emphasis on self-examination and moral introspection has significantly impacted moral philosophy and ethics. His belief that "an unexamined life is not worth living" continues to echo in contemporary discussions about the purpose and value of human life.

The criticisms and implications of Socratic philosophy highlight the richness and complexity of Socratic thought and its enduring relevance. They remind us that philosophy, in the Socratic sense, is not just an academic discipline but a way of life, a persistent pursuit of wisdom and moral understanding.

Chapter 3: Socratic Paradoxes

3.1 Defining Socratic Paradoxes

Socratic paradoxes refer to a set of provocative statements or beliefs attributed to Socrates in Plato's dialogues that seem contrary to common sense. These paradoxes are not paradoxes in the logical sense – they don't involve contradictions that defy resolution – but are statements that appear counterintuitive or contrary to accepted wisdom. They've been the subject of extensive analysis and debate among scholars.

Here are three well-known Socratic paradoxes:

No one does wrong knowingly (Socratic intellectualism): This paradox suggests that when individuals commit wrongful acts, they do so out of ignorance. Socrates posited that knowledge invariably leads to virtuous action, implying that immoral behavior is the result of misunderstanding or lack of knowledge (Plato,

Protagoras 352b-360d).

Virtue is knowledge: Socrates argued that virtues such as courage, temperance, and justice are forms of knowledge. Therefore, if one truly understands what is good, they will act accordingly. This is a distinctively intellectualist stance, placing knowledge at the heart of moral excellence (Plato, Meno 87e-89a).

All virtues are one: Often referred to as the unity of virtues, this paradox suggests that all virtues are interconnected and inseparable. One cannot have one virtue without having them all, as they all stem from wisdom, which is the highest form of knowledge (Plato, Protagoras 329b-333b).

These paradoxes are an integral part of Socratic philosophy. They challenged the conventional wisdom of the time and continue to provoke thought and debate. While they may seem contrary to common sense, each paradox offers insight into Socratic moral philosophy and his emphasis on the role of knowledge and intellectual rigor in the pursuit of a virtuous life.

3.2 Nobody Does Wrong Knowingly

The statement "Nobody does wrong knowingly" is one of the most famous Socratic paradoxes, and it's at the core of Socratic intellectualism. This paradox, in essence, asserts that when individuals engage in wrongful or immoral actions, they do so out of ignorance, not out of a willful desire to do wrong.

Socrates held a fundamentally optimistic view of human nature, believing that everyone inherently seeks the good. The problem arises when people mistake what is genuinely good for something that only appears good. According to Socrates, this misunderstanding is a form of intellectual error or ignorance. If people knew what was truly good, they would never choose to do wrong because doing so would contradict their fundamental desire for good.

This paradox radically shifts the perspective on wrongdoing from one of moral failure to one of intellectual error. It suggests that the remedy for immorality is not punishment, but education and enlightenment. If individuals truly understood the nature of good and evil, they would invariably choose the good. Hence, the focus of moral education should be on fostering understanding and wisdom, rather than instilling obedience through fear of punishment.

This notion has significant implications for ethics, legal theory, and education. It stresses the importance of knowledge and understanding in moral behavior and underlines the role of education in moral development. It also raises questions about moral responsibility and the nature of moral judgment, as it suggests that wrongful acts are the result of ignorance rather than malicious intent.

Despite being counterintuitive, the paradox "Nobody does wrong knowingly" offers a profound insight into Socratic moral philosophy and his belief in the transformative power of knowledge.

3.3 Virtue is Knowledge

The claim "Virtue is knowledge" is another

significant Socratic paradox that underpins Socratic ethics. According to Socrates, virtues such as courage, justice, and temperance are not just moral qualities, but forms of knowledge. This assertion forms the core of Socratic intellectualism (Plato, Meno 87e-89a)1.

Socrates believed that moral excellence is essentially an intellectual achievement. If one genuinely understands what is good, they would naturally act accordingly. In other words, knowing the right thing to do invariably leads to doing the right thing.

One example of this view can be seen in the dialogue "Meno," where Socrates suggests that virtues such as courage are not merely about fearlessness in the face of danger, but rather understanding what is truly worth fearing and what isn't. This requires wisdom, or knowledge, which elevates it from mere bravery to a virtue.

This perspective on virtue has profound implications for ethics and moral education. If virtue is indeed a form of knowledge, then moral education should be focused on fostering understanding and wisdom rather than merely instilling rules and norms. This intellectualist view also implies that moral error is a form of ignorance, echoing the paradox that "nobody does wrong knowingly."

However, this paradox has been the subject of extensive debate. Critics argue that it's possible for individuals to know what is right yet still choose to do wrong, suggesting a separation between moral knowledge and moral action. Despite these criticisms, the paradox "Virtue is knowledge" remains a central tenet of Socratic philosophy, highlighting the importance of wisdom and intellectual rigor in the pursuit of a virtuous life.

3.4 Virtue is the Highest Form of Good

Socrates held the belief that virtue is the highest form of good, a conviction that was foundational to his ethical theory. He maintained that leading a virtuous life is the most important and valuable pursuit, superseding all other forms of goods such as wealth, power, or bodily pleasure.

According to Socrates, virtues like justice, temperance, and wisdom are not only valuable in themselves but also contribute to a good and fulfilled life. These virtues are intrinsically good, and their value is not contingent on external circumstances or outcomes. This is in contrast to other goods such as wealth or power, which Socrates considered valuable only if used wisely and justly.

Socrates' belief that virtue is the highest form of good also informs his paradoxes "virtue is knowledge" and "no one does wrong knowingly". If virtue is indeed the ultimate good, it follows that knowing what is good (i.e., possessing virtue as knowledge) leads one to choose virtuous actions. Misdeeds, according to this view, are due to a lack of understanding about the true nature of goodness.

This conviction underlines Socrates' view of the purpose of human life, which he believed should be devoted to moral improvement and the pursuit of virtue. His famous assertion that "an unexamined life is not worth living" underscores this belief in the importance of self-reflection, wisdom, and moral excellence.

Socrates' assertion that virtue is the highest form of good encourages us to consider the nature of the good life, the value of moral excellence, and the role of wisdom in guiding our actions. It is a profound reflection on the importance of character and ethical understanding in our pursuit of happiness and fulfillment.

Chapter 4: Socrates and Politics

4.1 Political Stance and Athenian Politics

Socrates' political stance was both complex and controversial, shaping his interactions with the political landscape of Athens and ultimately playing a role in his trial and execution. While he was often skeptical of the prevailing democratic practices in Athens, he also demonstrated a deep commitment to the city and its laws.

Socrates' political philosophy was intrinsically linked to his broader philosophical outlook. His belief in the importance of wisdom and virtue shaped his view of ideal governance. He was critical of Athenian democracy because he felt that it allowed unqualified individuals to hold positions of power. In his view, only those with sufficient wisdom and knowledge should lead, echoing his conviction that "virtue is knowledge".

However, Socrates himself refrained from actively participating in politics. He explained that his divine mission, communicated through his inner daimonion, was to philosophize and examine life, not to engage in political affairs (Plato, Apology 31c-32a)3. Despite this, he fulfilled his duties as a citizen, including serving as a hoplite (soldier) in military campaigns and as a member of the boule (council) of Athens.

His criticisms of Athenian politics, combined with his unconventional behavior and teachings, often put him at odds with the Athenian political establishment. This tension culminated in his trial and execution, accused of impiety and corrupting the youth, which many interpreters see as a veiled criticism of his political views.

Despite his criticisms, Socrates demonstrated a deep respect for the law, insisting on abiding by the verdict of his trial rather than escaping from prison, emphasizing his commitment to the polis even in the face of death.

Socrates' political stance, characterized by his critical yet committed relationship with Athenian politics, offers valuable insights into the intersection of philosophy and politics, highlighting the role of wisdom, virtue, and critical reflection in the pursuit of just governance.

4.2 Critique of Democracy

While Socrates lived in one of the earliest democracies in history, he harbored significant criticisms of Athenian democratic practices. His critique was not against the principle of democracy itself, but rather the unguided application of it, which he saw as a potential pathway to mob rule or tyranny.

In the dialogue "The Republic," Socrates used the metaphor of a ship to illustrate his critique of democracy. He compared the citizens to sailors quarreling over the helm, with no understanding of navigation, yet believing they are equally entitled to steer. He pointed out the absurdity of appointing a ship's captain by lot or by persuasion, rather than by knowledge and expertise in navigation.

Socrates held that just as the skill of navigation is crucial for effectively steering a ship, wisdom and knowledge of the good are essential for governing a city. By letting anyone, regardless of their wisdom or moral understanding, participate in ruling, Athenian democracy risked making decisions that were not grounded in knowledge or guided by virtue.

Socrates also expressed concern that democracy can easily slide into demagoguery, where leaders manipulate the public's desires and emotions for their own gain rather than the common good.

Despite these critiques, it's crucial to note that Socrates was not advocating for any form of elitist or autocratic rule. His vision of ideal governance, often referred to as the philosopher-kingship, called for rulers who have a profound understanding of justice and the good, and who rule not for personal gain, but for the welfare of the polis.

Socrates' critique of democracy urges us to

reflect on the nature of political power, the role of wisdom in governance, and the potential pitfalls of unchecked democratic practices.

4.3 Impact on Athenian Democracy

Despite his criticism of Athenian democracy and avoidance of direct political involvement, Socrates had a profound impact on the political consciousness of Athens. His philosophical interrogations and the manner of his death posed critical challenges to Athenian democratic values and practices, influencing both his contemporaries and future generations.

Socrates' method of philosophical inquiry, known as the Socratic Method, encouraged critical thinking and self-reflection. By questioning accepted beliefs and norms, he fostered a spirit of intellectual rigor and skepticism among Athenian citizens. This contributed to a more vibrant and reflective democratic discourse, fostering the idea that democratic participation should involve thoughtful deliberation rather than unexamined consensus.

Moreover, Socrates' trial and execution posed a significant challenge to Athenian democracy. It revealed the potential for democratic processes to be used unjustly, and it showed that the will of the majority does not always equate to justice or truth. His execution is often seen as a reflection of the intolerance of Athenian democracy towards dissent and unconventional ideas, sparking debates about the limits of democratic freedom and the importance of protecting minority views.

In the aftermath of Socrates' death, there was a sense of regret among some Athenians, leading to a posthumous exoneration. His death served as a stark reminder of the potential dangers of unchecked majority rule and the necessity of protecting individual rights and freedoms within a democratic society.

Socrates' impact on Athenian democracy extends far beyond his lifetime. His philosophical approach continues to inform democratic values such as freedom of speech, critical thinking, and individual rights. His life and death serve as a potent reminder of the potential pitfalls of democracy and the importance of intellectual rigor and moral integrity in political life.

4.4 Trial and Execution: A Democratic Verdict

The trial and execution of Socrates in 399 BC represents a pivotal moment in the history of Athenian democracy. The democratic processes that led to his conviction and death sentence reflect the complex interplay between individual rights, democratic decision-making, and societal norms.

Socrates was charged with impiety and corrupting the youth, accusations that reflected broader concerns about his influence on Athenian society and politics. His public criticism of democratic processes and his practice of questioning traditional beliefs were seen as threatening to the established order.

His trial was conducted in a democratic manner, with a jury of 501 Athenian citizens selected by lot. Socrates was given the opportunity to defend himself, a fundamental aspect of Athenian legal proceedings that ensured the accused's right to a fair hearing. Despite this, the verdict reached by the jury represents a contentious example of majority rule.

Socrates' defense, as depicted in Plato's "Apology," was unyielding and defiant. He reaffirmed his philosophical mission and refused to apologize for his actions. When offered the chance to propose an alternative sentence, he suggested free maintenance by the state, a suggestion that further angered the jury. Ultimately, the democratic assembly voted for his execution.

The decision to execute Socrates can be viewed as a democratic verdict in the sense that it was reached through democratic processes. However, it also exposed the potential for such processes to infringe upon individual freedoms and to suppress dissenting voices.

Socrates' trial and execution remain subjects of ongoing debate, raising questions about the nature of justice, the limits of democratic decision-making, and the value of dissent within a democratic society. His story serves as a powerful reminder of the need for democratic systems to safeguard individual rights and to protect the freedom to question and challenge established beliefs and norms.

Chapter 5: Socrates and His Influence

5.1 Socrates and Plato: Profound Influence

The profound influence of Socrates on Plato cannot be overstated. As his student, Plato spent several years in close proximity to Socrates, absorbing his teachings and witnessing firsthand his philosophical methods. This relationship significantly shaped Plato's thought, marking him as one of the primary conduits through which we have come to understand Socrates.

Plato's dialogues, many of which feature Socrates as the main interlocutor, are among our primary sources for understanding Socratic philosophy. Plato used the dialogues not only to document Socrates' teachings and methods but also as a platform for developing his own philosophical ideas. As such, the Socratic voice in these dialogues often serves a dual purpose: it captures the spirit of Socrates while simultaneously articulating Plato's evolving thoughts.

Socrates' method of inquiry, commonly known as the Socratic Method, heavily influenced Plato's dialectic approach. Plato adopted and refined this method, using it as a powerful tool for examining and elucidating philosophical concepts 4.

Moreover, Socrates' moral philosophy, with its emphasis on the intrinsic worth of virtue and the pursuit of the good life, formed the foundation of Plato's ethical thought. Ideas such as the unity of virtues, the claim that no one does evil knowingly, and the notion that virtue is the highest good all originate from Socratic teachings and are central to Plato's ethics.

Finally, Socrates' trial and execution had a profound impact on Plato. This experience cemented Plato's disillusionment with Athenian politics and spurred his exploration of justice and the ideal state in his later works, most notably in "The Republic".

The legacy of Socrates is thus deeply interwoven with Plato's philosophical journey. As teacher and student their intellectual relationship has left an indelible mark on the history of Western philosophy.

5.2 The Platonic Socrates

The "Platonic Socrates" refers to the portrayal of Socrates in Plato's dialogues. This version of Socrates is the primary lens through which we understand his philosophical teachings and methodology. However, it's crucial to note that the Platonic Socrates may not entirely represent the historical figure. Instead, he often serves as a philosophical character through which Plato explores and develops his own ideas.

The Platonic Socrates is best known for his use of the Socratic Method, a form of inquiry that involves asking probing questions to expose the contradictions in one's beliefs and to stimulate critical thinking. This method of dialectic conversation plays a pivotal role in most Platonic dialogues and has become synonymous with Socratic philosophy.

In terms of ethical teachings, the Platonic Socrates advocates for the intrinsic worth of virtue and the idea that knowledge is the pathway to moral goodness. He asserts that "no one does wrong knowingly" and that "virtue is knowledge" - two Socratic paradoxes that feature prominently in Plato's dialogues.

The Platonic Socrates also frequently discusses the nature of the soul and the importance of caring for one's soul above all else. He often engages in discussions about the immortality of the soul, particularly in dialogues like "Phaedo" and "Phaedrus".

It's important to remember that while the Platonic Socrates provides valuable insights into Socratic philosophy, it may not fully encapsulate the real Socrates. The figure of Socrates in Plato's works is both a historical persona and a philosophical tool, serving as a conduit through which Plato explores philosophical questions and articulates his philosophical vision.

5.3 Xenophon's Recollection

Xenophon, an Athenian general, historian, and a contemporary of Socrates, offers a different perspective on Socrates in his works. Like Plato, Xenophon was a student of Socrates and his works provide valuable insights into Socrates' life and philosophy. However, his portrayal of Socrates, often termed as "Xenophontic Socrates," differs significantly from the "Platonic Socrates."

Xenophon's most notable work concerning Socrates is the "Memorabilia," which presents Socrates not so much as a speculative philosopher but as a sage and a moral exemplar. According to Xenophon, Socrates was a practical man who was more concerned with ethical and social matters than metaphysical speculations.

In Xenophon's portrayal, Socrates appears to be less confrontational and ironical compared to the version we see in Plato's dialogues. Instead, he comes across as a more accessible, straightforward teacher, guiding his friends and followers on matters of practical ethics and good living.

Notably, Xenophon presents Socrates as a staunch defender of conventional morality and Athenian law, which contrasts with Plato's portrayal of Socrates as a critic of established norms. Xenophon's Socrates emphasizes loyalty to friends, respect for authorities, and practical wisdom in daily life.

Moreover, in "Apology," Xenophon recounts Socrates' trial and death, providing an alternative account to Plato's. Xenophon's account underscores Socrates' calm acceptance of his fate and his unwavering commitment to his philosophical mission.

Xenophon's portrayal of Socrates, while it may diverge from the Socrates we know through Plato, provides a complementary perspective that enriches our understanding of this complex figure. His works remind us of the multifaceted nature of Socrates' philosophy and character, and the myriad ways he left his mark on his contemporaries and subsequent generations.

5.4 Differences Between Xenophon and Plato's Accounts

While both Plato and Xenophon were students of Socrates and dedicated significant parts of their works to his philosophy, their portrayals of their teacher differ in significant ways, each reflecting their individual interests and philosophical inclinations.

Philosophical Depth: Plato's Socrates is seen as a profound and complex philosophical character, engaged in deep metaphysical speculations and ethical dilemmas. He is seen discussing the nature of knowledge, virtue, and the soul, among other philosophical topics. Conversely, Xenophon's Socrates is more straightforward, practical, and moralistic, focusing more on advice for good living and practical ethics.

Socratic Method: Plato emphasizes the Socratic Method, a form of inquiry involving relentless questioning to expose contradictions in beliefs. This method features prominently in Plato's dialogues. Xenophon's Socrates, on the other hand, is seen less frequently engaging in this form of dialogue. Instead, he is often portrayed as imparting wisdom and advice to his friends.

Attitude towards Athenian Society: In Plato's

dialogues, Socrates is often portrayed as a critic of conventional beliefs and societal norms. He questions the established moral and political order, leading to tensions with the Athenian authorities. In contrast, Xenophon's Socrates is depicted as a supporter of traditional morality and conventional norms, presenting him as a less controversial figure.

Accounts of the Trial: In their accounts of Socrates' trial, Plato's "Apology" depicts Socrates as a defiant figure, maintaining his philosophical stance even in the face of death. Xenophon's "Apology," in contrast, emphasizes Socrates' calm acceptance of his fate and his steadfast belief in the Delphic oracle.

These differences, while significant, do not necessarily denote contradictions but rather reflect the multifaceted character of Socrates as seen through the eyes of two of his most famous students. Both accounts, despite their differences, contribute to a richer, more nuanced understanding of Socrates' philosophy and persona.

Chapter 6: Socrates and Religion

6.1 Socrates' Views on Religion

Religion played a significant role in the life and philosophy of Socrates, as it did in the lives of most ancient Greeks. However, understanding Socrates' views on religion is complex due to the nature of our sources. Most of our information about his beliefs comes from the works of Plato and Xenophon, each of whom may have presented Socrates in ways that align with their own philosophical perspectives.

Despite these challenges, it's generally agreed that Socrates believed in the gods of the Greek pantheon, as was common in Athens during his time. Yet, his religious views were unconventional in certain ways and led to misunderstanding and suspicion among his contemporaries.

Socrates often claimed to be guided by a divine

sign or voice, referred to as his "daimonion." This inner voice, he asserted, never directed his actions but only warned him against certain actions. This daimonion was a unique aspect of his belief system and was part of the charges against him during his trial.

According to the Platonic dialogues, Socrates held that the gods are completely good and hence could not cause harm or evil, which was contrary to the popular Greek mythology that often portrayed gods as capricious and morally ambiguous. This belief likely contributed to the charge of impiety leveled against him.

In Xenophon's accounts, Socrates is portrayed as a pious man who believed in fulfilling religious obligations and participating in public sacrifices. Yet, he also appeared to hold the gods at an intellectual distance, advocating for rational inquiry over blind faith.

It's important to note that the charges of impiety against Socrates during his trial were likely politically motivated and indicative of the societal unrest of the time, rather than a fair reflection of his religious beliefs. Nonetheless, the unconventional elements of Socrates' religious views continue to intrigue scholars and contribute to the rich complexity of his philosophical legacy.

6.2 Charges of Impiety

Impiety (asebeia in Greek) was a serious charge in ancient Athens, where religion permeated all aspects of public and private life. In 399 BCE, Socrates was accused of impiety, a charge that ultimately led to his trial and execution. The indictment, as presented by his accuser Meletus, was twofold: first, that Socrates did not believe in the gods of the state, and second, that he introduced new deities.

The charge of disbelief in the state gods was probably linked to Socrates' critical attitude towards traditional beliefs and mythology. In various Platonic dialogues, Socrates is seen challenging conventional representations of the gods, particularly the notion that they could be responsible for evil or immoral acts. These views may have been seen as undermining the state religion.

The accusation of introducing new deities refers to Socrates' claim of being guided by his "daimonion," a sort of divine voice or sign that warned him against certain actions. This was not a deity in the traditional sense, but his accusers might have interpreted it as such. This personal, internal "divine sign" was unique to Socrates and deviated from common religious experiences.

In his defense, Socrates argued that he did believe in gods, and thus the charges of atheism were unfounded. He also contended that his daimonion did not constitute a new deity but was a personal spiritual experience, which should not be considered impious.

The charges of impiety, it should be noted, were likely politically motivated. Socrates was a prominent figure associated with the intellectual elite, some of whom had fallen out of favor in the aftermath of the Peloponnesian War. His trial can be seen as part of the political and social turbulence of the time.

Despite his arguments, Socrates was found guilty by the jury and sentenced to death, cementing his place as a martyr for philosophy and freedom of thought.

6.3 The "Divine Sign"

The "divine sign" (daimonion) is a distinct aspect of Socrates' personal belief system. Frequently mentioned in Plato's dialogues, this inner voice or spiritual guide is unique to Socrates and a central part of his philosophical practice.

According to Socrates, this inner voice did not instruct him on what to do, but rather warned him against certain actions, particularly those that might lead to moral error. It remained silent when his actions were morally correct.

In Plato's "Euthyphro," Socrates states that this divine sign had dissuaded him from having any considerable involvement in politics, as it would have led to his premature death. This indicates that the divine sign guided Socrates in maintaining his philosophical integrity.

The nature and origin of the daimonion remain a subject of speculation among scholars. It is often seen as a reflection of Socrates' profound moral consciousness and commitment to ethical conduct. Some interpret it as an expression of Socratic irony, while others suggest it reflects Socrates' deep intuition.

Notably, the divine sign contributed to the charges against Socrates at his trial. His accusers interpreted it as the introduction of new gods, a serious charge in the context of Athenian religious customs. In response, Socrates maintained that his divine sign was not a separate deity, but a form of divine communication.

Despite the controversy it generated, the daimonion remains a powerful symbol of Socrates' commitment to individual conscience and moral discernment, principles that lie at the heart of his philosophical legacy.

6.4 Impact on Greek Religious Thought

Socrates' unique approach to religion, despite landing him in conflict with his society, had profound implications for Greek religious thought and, by extension, the development of

Western philosophy.

Ethical Monotheism: Socrates, as depicted in the Platonic dialogues, promoted the idea that the gods are completely good and incapable of evil. This ethical conception of the divine was in stark contrast to the traditional Greek mythology, which portrayed gods with human-like flaws and moral failings. This may be seen as a step towards "ethical monotheism," a belief system that would later be central to many Western religions.

Religion and Morality: Socrates questioned the traditional Greek view that morality derives from the gods. He argued that something is not pious merely because the gods love it, but rather the gods love it because it is pious. This viewpoint divorced morality from divine will and suggested an independent moral order.

Rational Inquiry and Religion: Socrates applied rational inquiry and philosophical investigation to religious beliefs and practices, an approach that was uncommon in ancient Greece. This critical examination paved the way for future philosophical and theological debates about the nature of the divine and the relationship between faith and reason.

Personal Religious Experience: Socrates' "daimonion" or inner divine voice could be seen as an early representation of personal religious experience. His belief in this individual spiritual guidance system, despite being misunderstood in his own time, might have opened up new ways of understanding the divine-human interaction, emphasizing the role of individual conscience.

Despite his execution for alleged impiety, Socrates' approach to religion had a lasting impact. His application of philosophical inquiry to the realm of religion, his unique conception of the divine, and his emphasis on personal moral responsibility all contributed to shifts in religious thinking in the centuries that followed.

Chapter 7: The Ethics of Socrates

7.1 Socratic Ethics Defined

Socratic ethics represents a paradigm shift in ancient Greek thought. Prior to Socrates, moral values were primarily derived from traditional narratives, such as myths, and societal conventions. Socrates, however, sought to ground ethical principles in reason and dialogue, which became a hallmark of Western philosophy.

Socratic ethics is primarily known through the dialogues of his student, Plato. Socrates himself left no written works. Here are the key components of Socratic ethics as inferred from these sources:

Intellectualism: Socratic intellectualism posits that nobody does wrong knowingly and that all wrongdoing arises from ignorance. In other words, if a person truly knows what is good, they will act accordingly. This principle suggests that moral knowledge is the most important type of knowledge, as it leads to virtuous actions.

Virtue is Knowledge: Following from Socratic intellectualism, Socrates argued that virtue is a form of knowledge and can be taught. This view contrasts with the traditional Greek belief that virtues such as courage and temperance were innate qualities.

Eudaimonism: Socrates believed that virtue leads to eudaimonia, often translated as "happiness" or "flourishing." He argued that leading a virtuous life aligns with our true self-interest and leads to a fulfilled and meaningful life.

The Unity of Virtues: Socrates proposed that virtues are not separate qualities but rather interconnected aspects of a single underlying good. For instance, one cannot be truly courageous without also being just, and vice versa.

The Socratic Paradoxes: Socratic ethics is also

characterized by several paradoxical claims, such as "I know that I know nothing," which reflects his commitment to intellectual humility and the constant pursuit of knowledge.

While these principles might seem simple, their implications are profound and far-reaching. Socratic ethics remains a vibrant field of study and continues to influence philosophical thought on morality and human behavior.

7.2 The Role of Reason in Ethics

Socrates, often seen as the progenitor of Western philosophy, conferred upon reason a paramount role in ethics. This rationality-centered approach to morality is distinct from the traditional norms of his time, where ethics were primarily defined by societal customs and mythological narratives.

In Socratic ethics, reason is depicted as the instrumental faculty enabling us to apprehend what is genuinely good, thereby influencing our actions. This Socratic assertion—that reason defines moral behavior—runs counter to the prevailing idea that individuals willingly engage in harmful actions. Instead, Socrates insisted that such behavior stemmed from ignorance, a lack of knowledge, and that, given true understanding, individuals would naturally gravitate toward virtuous actions. As expressed in Plato's "Protagoras," Socrates posits, "No one who either knows or believes that there is another possible course of action, better than the one he is taking, will continue on his present course"[1].

The elenchus, or the Socratic method, exemplifies reason's practical application within the realm of ethics. This method involves a rigorous questioning process designed to dissect the consistency and credibility of one's beliefs. In employing this conversational approach, Socrates aimed to uncover ethical truths and dispel ignorance. In the "Meno," he guides Meno through a series of questions to demonstrate that virtue is a form of knowledge and can be taught. Socrates asserts, "There will be no end to the troubles of states, or of humanity itself, till philosophers become kings in this world, or till those we now call kings and rulers really and truly become philosophers".

The interplay between reason and ethics in Socratic philosophy underscores the individual's responsibility in ethical decision-making. Socrates believed that morality wasn't dictated by external societal norms but was a result of internal rational deliberation. This idea of individual responsibility is evident in "Crito," where Socrates rejects Crito's plea for escape by stating, "One should value the good opinions, and not the bad ones...of the sensible and just"3. This dialog establishes Socratic allegiance to the laws of Athens—illustrating that the rational and morally correct course isn't always the easiest.

By intertwining reason with ethical conduct, Socrates inaugurated a method of inquiry-driven approach to morality. His teachings fostered the practice of critically examining one's beliefs—an idea that became fundamental to Western philosophical tradition.

7.3 Virtue Ethics

Socrates' approach to ethics has played a foundational role in what we now call virtue ethics, a branch of moral philosophy that emphasizes character over rules or consequences. As with other aspects of his philosophy, Socrates' views on virtue were not documented by Socrates himself but have been inferred from the dialogues of his student, Plato, and the writings of Xenophon, another of his contemporaries.

In the "Meno," Socrates investigates the nature of virtue and whether it can be taught. He challenges Meno's attempts to define virtue as a set of specific actions or behaviors associated with different roles in society. Instead, Socrates argues that virtues like justice, wisdom, courage, and temperance are all aspects of a single concept of the good. This idea, known as the unity of virtues, forms an essential part of Socratic virtue ethics.

Socrates posits that virtue equates to knowledge of the good. If one truly understands what is good, one will act virtuously. Conversely, if one fails to act virtuously, it is because of a lack of knowledge, a principle referred to as Socratic intellectualism. This principle is famously expressed in the Socratic paradox: "No one errs or does wrong willingly or knowingly."

Socratic virtue ethics is inherently eudaimonistic, as it postulates that living a virtuous life leads to eudaimonia, a term often translated as "happiness" or "flourishing." According to Socrates, eudaimonia isn't achieved by pursuing wealth or status but by cultivating virtue3. This view is expressed in his statement in the "Apology": "The unexamined life is not worth living."

Socrates' exploration of virtue and his insistence on the intrinsic value of a virtuous life have profoundly influenced the development of ethical thought. His focus on character and moral integrity over mere obedience to rules or laws remains a cornerstone of virtue ethics.

7.4 The Socratic Conception of Happiness

The concept of happiness, or eudaimonia, is a significant aspect of Socrates' ethical framework. Unlike many modern interpretations of happiness, which often associate the term with transient pleasure or material prosperity, Socrates envisioned eudaimonia as a comprehensive state of well-being or flourishing intertwined with the practice of moral virtue.

In the Socratic philosophical perspective, happiness isn't purely a state of subjective emotional satisfaction. It is an objective condition of the soul attained through an incessant pursuit of knowledge and moral virtue. This standpoint presents a stark contrast with the hedonistic emphasis on physical pleasure as the ultimate good, as propagated by ancient Greek philosophical schools such as the Cyrenaics and Epicureans.

For Socrates, moral integrity and intellectual enlightenment are the cornerstones of genuine happiness, rather than external goods or social recognition. This belief prominently surfaces in the "Apology," wherein Socrates, addressing the court, asserts, "Are you not ashamed of caring so much for the making of money and for fame and prestige, when you neither think nor care about wisdom and truth and the improvement of your soul?". This bold statement indicates a subversion of traditional Athenian norms, positing that wealth and reputation are meaningless without the underpinning of virtuous conduct.

Further exposition on Socratic happiness can be found in the "Gorgias," where he delves into the dichotomy between the desires of the body and those of the soul3. Bodily desires—those related to physical gratification, such as food, drink, and sensual pleasures—can offer ephemeral joy but fail to contribute to lasting happiness. In contrast, the desires of the soul—those that relate to the pursuit of knowledge, wisdom, and virtue—facilitate a deeper, enduring form of satisfaction. Socrates states, "For I assert that the just man and the pious, the wise man and the man truly so, stand a better chance of doing well and being happy than those who are not."

This understanding of happiness as the outcome of virtuous living has been profoundly influential in the evolution of Western ethical thought. Plato and Aristotle, among others, extended Socratic eudaimonistic ethics by rooting their philosophical systems in the pursuit of the supreme good, manifested in a life characterized by virtue and intellectual fulfilment.

Chapter 8: Socrates in Subsequent Philosophical Thought

8.1 Socrates in Hellenistic Philosophy

The figure of Socrates looms large in Hellenistic philosophy, despite the fact that Socrates himself predates the Hellenistic era (323-31 BCE). The influence of his philosophical ideas and methodologies was profound and lasting, and his teachings laid the groundwork for many of the Hellenistic schools of thought.

For the Stoics, a school of philosophy that emphasized rationalism and self-control as the path to virtue, Socrates was seen as an exemplar of Stoic values. His resilience and equanimity in the face of adversity, as well as his commitment to moral and intellectual integrity, were qualities greatly admired by Stoic philosophers such as Epictetus, who is recorded to have said, "The first and greatest task of the philosopher is to test and separate appearances, and to act on nothing that is untested".

The Epicureans, although in many ways divergent from the Stoic philosophy, still found value in Socratic thought. Epicurus himself admired Socrates' skill in logical argumentation and his disdain for the sophists, despite holding different views on the purpose of philosophy and the highest good. Epicurus taught that pleasure was the highest good, a position that contrasted with Socrates' virtue-focused eudaimonism. However, he echoed Socrates in asserting that philosophy's purpose was to secure the well-being of the soul.

In the Sceptic tradition, which emerged from the teachings of Pyrrho of Elis, we see a different sort of Socratic influence. Pyrrho is said to have been influenced by the "Socratic ignorance," the idea expressed by Socrates that he knew only that he knew nothing. This led to a form of philosophical skepticism, advocating the suspension of judgment due to the unreliability of sensory perception and the insufficiency of our knowledge.

While the philosophers of the Hellenistic period had divergent views and pursued their own unique philosophical projects, they were united in their admiration for Socrates. His philosophical methodologies, his approach to ethics, and his emphasis on the importance of a virtuous life all deeply impacted these subsequent schools of thought.

8.2 Socrates in Medieval Philosophy

The Middle Ages, or the Medieval period (approximately 5th to the 15th century), presented a significant shift in the cultural and philosophical landscape, particularly with the rise of Christianity and the church's domination over intellectual discourse. Despite this shift, Socrates, an icon of ancient Greek philosophy, made his presence felt in the tapestry of Medieval philosophy, largely through the writings of early Church Fathers and later Scholastic philosophers.

A significant moment in this period was the encounter of Christian thought with Greek philosophy, facilitated by philosophers like Augustine of Hippo, who relied heavily on the Platonic tradition1. As Plato's dialogues were our primary source of information about Socrates, Socratic ideas came to be discussed, albeit indirectly, within this context. Augustine admired the Socratic focus on moral and intellectual self-improvement and the idea of the immortality of the soul, which had clear resonances with Christian thought.

During the period known as Scholasticism (approximately 12th to 15th century), Aristotelian philosophy held sway, but Socratic influence could still be detected. Thomas Aquinas, for instance, in his voluminous works, made use of the Socratic method of questioning and examination to elucidate complex theological and philosophical concepts.

In the writings of these and other medieval philosophers, Socrates was often portrayed as a kind of pagan precursor to Christian values and ideals. His emphasis on virtue, his faith in a divine moral order, his piety, and even his martyr-like death all resonated with Christian themes.

Moreover, the figure of Socrates served as a bridge between faith and reason, two concepts often in tension during the Middle Ages. His philosophical method, which invited rigorous questioning and logical examination, was a powerful tool that some medieval thinkers used to support or challenge religious teachings.

By the end of the Middle Ages, as the Renaissance began to dawn, the rediscovery and translation of many Greek texts resulted in a renewed interest in Socrates. His philosophical approach, ethical teachings, and unique persona continued to inspire thinkers, setting the stage for further exploration in the centuries to come.

8.3 Socrates in Modern and Contemporary Philosophy

As the era of Modern philosophy dawned, the Socratic figure continued to exert a considerable influence. Across the centuries, the person of Socrates, as well as his philosophical method and teachings, have been drawn upon, reinterpreted, and often reimagined to suit the particular concerns of the times.

The Enlightenment thinkers, for instance, found in Socrates a champion of reason and free inquiry. Voltaire, one of the luminaries of the Enlightenment, praised Socrates as "the first of mortals who discussed laws, physics, and morality".

Immanuel Kant, the giant of modern philosophy, echoed Socratic emphasis on morality being grounded in reason and the universal applicability of moral laws. His categorical imperative — the idea that moral duty should guide our actions regardless of our desires or consequences — can be seen as a reworking of Socratic ideas within a modern philosophical framework.

In the 19th century, Socrates' figure was a subject of deep fascination for the existentialist philosophers. For Friedrich Nietzsche, Socrates represented the dialectician par excellence but also the embodiment of a life-denying rationality that negates life's instinctual and creative aspects (Nietzsche, The Birth of Tragedy, 1872)3. For Kierkegaard, Socrates was the "master ironist" whose method serves as a form of indirect communication to encourage individuals to think for themselves.

Socratic influence is also discernible in the 20th-century philosophical landscape. For instance, the philosopher Karl Popper reinterpreted the Socratic method as a form of critical rationalism, a philosophical approach that emphasizes the importance of questioning and criticism in the pursuit of knowledge.

Today, the spirit of Socrates continues to pervade contemporary philosophy. His relentless questioning, intellectual honesty, and commitment to the examined life remain touchstones of philosophical inquiry. Whether in ethics, political philosophy, philosophy of mind, or other domains, the echoes of Socratic thought are never too distant, underscoring the timeless relevance of this singular philosopher.

8.4 The Global Reception of Socratic Thought

Socrates, as a defining figure in Western philosophy, has left a considerable imprint on global intellectual history. His philosophical approaches and teachings have found resonance across diverse cultures and philosophical traditions, sometimes being adapted and transformed in the process.

In East Asian thought, Confucianism and Neo-Confucianism bear striking parallels with Socratic ideas. Both Confucius and Socrates, for example, advocated for self-cultivation and moral virtue as the highest good. The Socratic method of questioning and dialogue also resembles the Confucian practice of 'rectification of names' - the insistence on clarity and accuracy in language for ethical and political correctness.

The Buddhist tradition, with its emphasis on the impermanence of the self and the pursuit of enlightenment, also finds echoes in Socratic philosophy. Notably, the Socratic idea of 'knowing oneself' and the Buddhist doctrine of 'self-realization' bear striking similarities, although interpreted within their unique cultural and philosophical contexts.

Socrates' impact is also seen in Middle Eastern thought, particularly during the Golden Age of Islamic philosophy (8th to 14th centuries), where his ideas were disseminated alongside those of Plato and Aristotle. The philosopher Al-Farabi, for instance, often cited Socratic thought in his discussions on political philosophy.

In Africa, the Socratic tradition of inquiry and debate has been likened to the practice of Ubuntu, a philosophy emphasizing communal dialogue and consensus. The emphasis Socrates placed on questioning and critical thinking finds resonance in the African tradition of 'learning through dialogue.'

Latin American philosophy, especially in its modern iterations, also bears the imprint of Socratic thought. For example, the emphasis on liberatory and critical pedagogy in the works of

Paulo Freire echoes the Socratic method's empowering and transformative nature.

In essence, Socrates' philosophical legacy has transcended geographical and cultural boundaries. His life and thought continue to inspire and provoke philosophical contemplation, affirming the universality of the human quest for wisdom and truth.

Chapter 9: Socrates in Art, Literature, and Popular Culture

9.1 Socrates in Ancient Art

Portrayals of Socrates in ancient art provide an essential visual supplement to the textual narratives of his life and teachings. These works, most of which date from the 5th and 4th centuries BCE, have been invaluable in deepening our understanding of the philosopher and the context in which he lived and thought.

One of the earliest known artistic depictions of Socrates can be found on pottery and vase paintings. These portrayals often depict Socrates in conversation with other Athenians, thereby illustrating his characteristic practice of public philosophy. Notably, Socrates is often shown as an ugly man, consistent with descriptions in the literary sources.

Another key depiction of Socrates is found in

the statue sculpted by Lysippos, a renowned Greek sculptor. While the original statue is lost, we know of it through Roman copies and literary references. The statue depicted Socrates as bald, stout, and unattractive — in contrast to the idealized beauty commonly found in Greek sculpture.

Additionally, the famous 'Death of Socrates' scene was a recurring motif in ancient art. A notable example is a Pompeiian wall painting, which portrays the philosopher's calm demeanor in his final moments, surrounded by his distraught disciples. This scene visually encapsulates Socratic virtues of courage and equanimity in the face of death.

One can also look to ancient coins for representations of Socrates. For instance, a 4th-century BCE bronze coin from the city of Aegina depicts Socrates on one side and a sea turtle — Aegina's emblem — on the other. These coins indicate the widespread recognition of Socrates' philosophical importance even outside Athens.

Altogether, these pieces of ancient art, while not numerous, have played a significant role in shaping our image of Socrates. They provide us a fascinating visual testimony of the enduring influence of this great philosopher in the ancient world.

9.2 Socrates in Literature

Socrates' influence extends well beyond the realm of philosophy and into the world of literature. His enduring presence across different literary genres and periods underlines the significance and the timelessness of his ideas.

In classical literature, the figure of Socrates has been presented both seriously and satirically. His contemporary, the comedic playwright Aristophanes, caricatured Socrates in his play 'The Clouds' as a sophist and a corrupter of the youth[1]. In stark contrast, Plato's philosophical dialogues and Xenophon's 'Memorabilia' provide a more respectful and serious portrayal, presenting Socrates as a sage whose life exemplified his philosophical principles.

In the middle ages, the story of Socrates, particularly his trial and execution, found its way into various moralistic and didactic texts. His courage and equanimity in facing death were seen as exemplifying Christian virtues of faith and patience[4].

In the modern period, Socrates appeared as a character in several philosophical novels. For instance, in Voltaire's 'Candide,' Socrates is lauded for his virtue and wisdom. In more contemporary literature, like 'The Last Days of Socrates' by Paul Johnson, Socrates' life and philosophy are reimagined and presented in a new light.

Socrates also features in numerous poems, ranging from ancient to contemporary. For instance, in John Keats's 'Sonnet to Homer,' Socrates is mentioned as a beacon of wisdom and moral courage. In contemporary poetry, such as Wisława Szymborska's 'Notes from a Nonexistent Himalayan Expedition,' the Socratic approach to knowledge and inquiry is invoked to convey a sense of humility and wonder8.

Thus, through different literary periods and across genres, the figure of Socrates has served as an enduring symbol of the quest for wisdom and virtue. His life and teachings continue to inspire, challenge, and captivate the minds of readers and writers alike.

9.3 Socrates in Modern Art, Film, and Television

The influence of Socrates has not been confined to ancient times; it continues to permeate modern art, film, and television, demonstrating the timeless relevance of his ideas and life story.

In modern art, Socrates has been the subject of many influential works. Jacques-Louis David's neoclassical painting "The Death of Socrates" (1787) is a notable example. This work depicts the final moments of Socrates, reinforcing the philosopher's stoicism and bravery in the face of death.

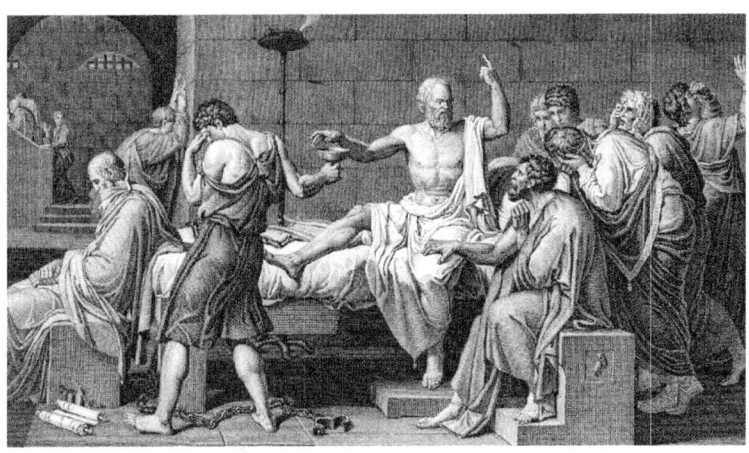

Socrates also appears as a motif in modern sculptures and public art installations, such as the bronze statue of Socrates in the Academy of Athens, which symbolizes his foundational role in Western philosophy.

In film, Socrates has been the subject of a range of productions. For example, the 1971 film "Socrates," directed by Roberto Rossellini, presents a dramatized account of the philosopher's life, focusing on his trial and execution. The 1988 film "The Last Temptation of Christ" by Martin Scorsese, though focused on Jesus, references Socrates in a dialogue that underscores the parallels between their lives and ideas.

In television, the figure of Socrates often appears in educational programming, documentaries, and animated series for children. Notably, in the popular animated series "Bill & Ted's Excellent Adventures," Socrates is depicted as an eccentric and wise figure who uses his questioning technique to humorous effect.

The Internet, too, has played a role in the modern reception of Socrates. From online philosophy courses to YouTube animations, Socrates and his philosophical ideas continue to engage a global audience.

Thus, in various media of the modern world, the figure of Socrates has remained an enduring symbol of wisdom, courage, and the ceaseless quest for truth.

9.4 The Popular Image of Socrates

Over the centuries, Socrates has transcended his historical context to become an icon of wisdom and intellectual inquiry in popular culture. The philosopher's influence pervades various aspects of society, from education to media, leaving a significant imprint on the collective consciousness.

In educational contexts, Socrates is often presented as the archetype of the philosopher. His method of questioning to probe the nature of knowledge and virtue has become a fundamental tool in pedagogical strategies, notably in the Socratic seminar method widely used in schools and universities.

In popular media, Socrates is frequently used as a symbol of wisdom, courage, and integrity. His name is often invoked in discussions of moral and ethical issues, reinforcing the continued relevance of his philosophical contributions.

The popular image of Socrates is also firmly established in everyday language and idioms. Phrases like 'Socratic questioning' and 'Socratic irony' are used to describe certain types of dialogue or conversational tactics, testifying to his lasting influence on the way we think and communicate.

In the world of digital technology and social media, Socrates is a recurrent figure. From memes that humorously reinterpret his ideas, to online philosophy forums that encourage Socratic debate, the philosopher's presence is evident in the digital sphere.

Yet, the popular image of Socrates is not

without its complexities. As with any historical figure of such magnitude, various interpretations coexist, leading to diverse and sometimes conflicting representations. While some view Socrates as the paragon of wisdom and virtue, others see him as a subversive figure, a critic of traditional values and institutions.

Regardless of these differences in perception, the widespread recognition of Socrates in popular culture testifies to the enduring relevance of his life and ideas. Through this wide array of representations, Socrates continues to encourage us to question, to seek knowledge, and to live a life of integrity and virtue.

Chapter 10: Evaluating Socrates: Historical and Philosophical Assessment

10.1 Historical Assessment

The assessment of Socrates from a historical perspective involves understanding not only his role as a thinker and a citizen of Athens but also his broader influence on the historical course of Western thought. Though Socrates left no writings of his own, his impact on subsequent generations—particularly through the accounts of his students—is undeniable.

Historically, Socrates is often seen as a pivotal figure in the transition from pre-Socratic philosophy, which largely focused on cosmological speculation, to classical philosophy, which emphasized moral and ethical questions. His method of philosophical inquiry laid the foundation for critical thinking and rational debate, contributing significantly to the intellectual tradition of the West.

As a citizen of Athens, Socrates lived during the city's golden age, but also its subsequent decline during the Peloponnesian War. The trial and execution of Socrates mark a significant turning point in Athenian history, symbolizing the tensions and conflicts within the democratic city-state.

Socrates' enduring influence on Western civilization is also seen in his role as a moral exemplar. His steadfast commitment to his principles—even in the face of death—resonates through the ages as a testament to intellectual integrity and moral courage.

Yet the historical assessment of Socrates is not without challenges. The absence of his personal writings and the reliance on secondary accounts—most notably those of Plato and Xenophon—has led to ongoing debates about the accuracy of the Socratic portrayal. Differing interpretations of these accounts have produced a 'Socratic problem,' concerning the true nature of Socratic philosophy.

Nevertheless, the influence of Socrates as a historical figure remains profound. Through his questioning method, his courage in the face of adversity, and his relentless pursuit of truth, Socrates has left an indelible mark on the historical trajectory of Western thought.

10.2 Influence on Western Philosophy

Socrates' influence on Western philosophy is hard to overstate. Known as the "father of Western philosophy", his approach to knowledge, ethics, and logic has shaped the trajectory of philosophical thought in profound ways.

Socrates' philosophical method, characterized by relentless questioning, has had a lasting impact on Western thought. The Socratic Method, as it is now known, has become a foundational aspect of philosophical inquiry and pedagogy. It not only promoted the development of logic and critical thinking, but also stressed the importance of self-knowledge, urging individuals to examine their own beliefs.

In the realm of ethics, Socrates' conviction that "virtue is knowledge" and that "the unexamined life is not worth living" set a new course for moral philosophy. His view that ethical knowledge was the highest form of understanding has reverberated through centuries of moral and ethical thought.

Socrates' influence can also be seen in his impact on his contemporaries and successors, particularly Plato, who was arguably his most famous student. Through Plato's dialogues, Socrates' philosophical ideas were passed on, deeply influencing Plato's own philosophy and the development of the Platonic tradition, including Neoplatonism.

Moreover, Socrates' impact extends beyond the field of philosophy. His thought has permeated other fields such as politics, where his critique of Athenian democracy has been a subject of much discussion. Similarly, in the fields of education, psychology, and law, Socratic questioning has been adapted as a means to promote critical thinking and deeper understanding.

Despite the passage of more than two millennia, the influence of Socrates on Western philosophy remains palpable. Through his unique method of inquiry, moral philosophy, and profound influence on subsequent thinkers, Socrates continues to be a central figure in the intellectual heritage of the West.

10.3 Socrates in Education

The influence of Socrates extends significantly into the field of education, shaping pedagogical strategies and ideals of learning. The legacy of Socratic thought is particularly visible in the concept of the "Socratic Method", a teaching approach centered on cooperative argumentative dialogue to stimulate critical thinking and illuminate ideas.

The Socratic Method's cornerstone is the concept of inquiry-based learning. Socrates believed that knowledge is innate and that it can be brought to consciousness through questioning. This concept has deeply influenced teaching methods across various disciplines, particularly in law, philosophy, and the humanities, where it encourages students to engage in analytical thinking, deepen their understanding, and learn to construct and defend their arguments.

Furthermore, Socrates' view on the purpose of education is echoed in many educational philosophies. He saw the aim of education as not merely to fill the minds of students with facts, but to cultivate virtue and critical thought. Socrates believed that an examined life—a life guided by self-reflection and personal growth—is the highest form of living. This idea has inspired educators to focus on developing students' abilities to think critically, reason ethically, and understand deeply.

The impact of Socratic ideals is also visible in educational ethics. Socrates' commitment to intellectual honesty and his courage in the pursuit of truth serve as an ethical model for educators and learners alike.

Despite the transformation of educational systems over the centuries, the influence of Socratic philosophy persists. The principles of Socratic questioning, the value placed on critical thinking, and the moral emphasis on the examined life continue to shape educational practices and ideals.

10.4 Relevance of Socratic Philosophy Today

Even after more than two millennia since his death, Socrates' philosophy continues to resonate with contemporary society, providing valuable insights and approaches in diverse areas of human life. From ethics to politics, and from education to personal growth, the timeless relevance of Socratic philosophy remains intact.

In the realm of ethics, Socrates' conviction that "virtue is knowledge" provides a timeless perspective on human behavior. It invites us to approach ethical issues not as a mere application of rules or laws, but as a pursuit of wisdom and understanding. This idea encourages reflection on our values, actions, and the ways in which our choices impact others.

In political discourse, Socrates' critique of democracy, particularly the dangers of ignorance and the manipulation of public opinion, remains particularly relevant. His questioning of Athenian democratic practices and the role of citizenry encourages us to scrutinize our own political systems and the nature of our participation in them.

The Socratic Method, with its emphasis on critical thinking and questioning, is more relevant than ever in an age overwhelmed by information and competing claims to truth. It offers a tool to navigate complex issues, encouraging dialogue, inquiry, and the examination of assumptions.

Socrates' concept of the 'examined life' continues to inspire the pursuit of self-understanding and personal growth. It underlines the significance of self-reflection in living a meaningful and fulfilling life, which is a concept embraced in contemporary psychotherapy and personal development strategies.

Furthermore, Socrates' conception of philosophy as a way of life rather than a mere academic discipline resonates with contemporary movements seeking to restore philosophy's practical and transformative dimensions.

In summary, the ideas and approaches put forth by Socrates remain deeply relevant, providing timeless wisdom in an ever-evolving world. By promoting critical thinking, ethical reflection, and personal growth, Socratic philosophy continues to enrich contemporary discourse and practice.

Glossary

Acrasia: A state of mind where someone acts against their better judgment due to weakness of will.

Acropolis: The fortified hill in the center of ancient Athens, known for its notable buildings and temples.

Agora: The central public space in ancient Greek city-states, typically used for assemblies and markets.

Alcibiades: A prominent Athenian statesman and general during the Peloponnesian War.

Anamnesis: In Plato's philosophy, a term describing the idea that knowledge is innate and 'recalled' from past incarnations.

Apologetic: In philosophy and theology, refers to the systematic argumentative discourse in defense of a doctrine.

Arete: In its basic sense, it means "excellence" of any kind. In the context of Greek ethics, your arete is tied to your fulfillment of purpose or function: the act of living up to one's full potential.

Aristocracy: A form of government in which power is held by the nobility.

Aristophanes: An ancient Greek playwright known for his satirical plays that often criticized social, political, and philosophical aspects of Athenian life.

Athenian Democracy: A system of government in which citizens participated directly in decision making, developed in the city-state of Athens in the 5th century BCE.

Cosmology: The study of the origin, evolution, and eventual fate of the universe.

Cynicism: A school of ancient Greek philosophy, advocating the rejection of conventional desires for wealth, power, and fame by living a simple life close to nature.

Daimonion: In the Socratic tradition, a type of inner voice or instinctual intuition that Socrates claimed to have as a life-guiding principle.

Delphic Oracle: The most important oracle in the classical Greek world, a priestess who prophesied under the influence of Apollo.

Dialectic: A method of argument for resolving disagreement, typically involving dialogue between two or more people holding different points of view.

Elenchus: The central technique of the Socratic method, an argumentative dialogue between individuals, based on asking and answering questions.

Epistemology: The study of knowledge, belief, and justified belief.

Eudaimonia: A central concept in Aristotelian ethics and political philosophy, often translated as "happiness" or "flourishing".

Hellenistic: Pertaining to the era and culture associated with the reign of Alexander the Great and his successors, characterized by the spread and fusion of Greek culture across the Mediterranean and Near East.

Hermeneutics: The theory and methodology of interpretation, especially the interpretation of biblical texts, wisdom literature, and philosophical texts.

Impiety: Disrespect towards god, religion, or anything held sacred.

Irony: A rhetorical device or form of humor involving a discrepancy between what is said and what is meant or is understood.

Metic: In ancient Athens, a resident alien that had some legal protections but did not have the same rights as citizens.

Oracle: In ancient Greece, a sacred place where deities were consulted about the future or certain courses of action, the responses often being given by an inspired priest or priestess.

Paradox: A seemingly self-contradictory statement or proposition that when investigated or explained may prove to be well-founded or true.

Peloponnesian War: A protracted conflict (431-404 BCE) between the city-states of Athens and Sparta, with each leading a coalition of allies.

Phronesis: An ancient Greek word for a type of wisdom or intelligence. It is more specifically a type of wisdom relevant to practical action, implying both good judgment and excellence of character and habits.

Platonic: Of, relating to, or characteristic of Plato or his philosophy.

Rhetoric: The art of effective or persuasive speaking or writing, especially the use of figures of speech and other compositional techniques.

Sophist: Itinerant intellectuals in ancient Greece who taught courses in various topics, including rhetoric, a kind of philosophy, and the interpretation of poetry.

Socratic Irony: A pose of ignorance assumed by Socrates in order to entice others into making statements that can then be challenged.

Socratic Method: The method of inquiry and discussion between individuals, based on asking and answering questions to stimulate critical thinking and illuminate ideas.

Sophrosyne: An ancient Greek concept of an ideal of excellence of character and soundness of mind, which when combined in one well-balanced individual leads to other qualities, such as temperance, moderation, prudence, purity, and self-control.

Stoicism: An ancient Greek school of philosophy that teaches the development of self-control and fortitude as a means of overcoming destructive emotions.

Symposium: A convivial meeting for drinking, music, and intellectual discussion among the ancient Greeks.

Thumos: In classical Greek philosophy, one part of the tripartite division of the soul attributed to Plato; it is the aspect associated with passion, spirit, or energy.

Tragedy: A form of drama based on human suffering that invokes an accompanying catharsis or pleasure in audiences.

Virtue Ethics: Class of normative ethical theories which treat the concept of moral virtue as central to ethics.

Xenophanes: Pre-Socratic philosopher who critiqued Homeric theology, distinguished the gods as fictions of the people, proposed a singular god of his own conception.

Xenophon: An ancient Greek philosopher, historian, soldier, and student of Socrates, known for recording many of Socrates' ideas in his works.

Further Reading

"The Trial and Death of Socrates" by Plato

"The Last Days of Socrates" by Plato

"Plato's Socrates" by Thomas C. Brickhouse and Nicholas D. Smith

"Socratic Wisdom: The Model of Knowledge in Plato's Early Dialogues" by Hugh H. Benson

"Socrates: A Man for Our Times" by Paul Johnson

"Socratic Studies" by Gregory Vlastos

"The Philosophy of Socrates" edited by Thomas C. Brickhouse and Nicholas D. Smith

"Socrates and Legal Obligation" by Roslyn Weiss

"Socrates in the City: Conversations on Life, God, and Other Small Topics" by Eric Metaxas

"Socratic Puzzles" by Robert Nozick

"The Cambridge Companion to Socrates" edited by Donald R. Morrison

"The Philosophy of Socrates: A Collection of Critical Essays" edited by Gregory Vlastos

"Socratic Moral Psychology" by Thomas C. Brickhouse and Nicholas D. Smith

"Socratic Charis: Philosophy without the Agon" by Drew A. Hyland

"Socrates: Ironist and Moral Philosopher" by Gregory Vlastos

"Socrates and Alcibiades: Four Texts" edited by Hans-Johann Glock

"Socrates Dissatisfied: An Analysis of Plato's Crito" by Roslyn Weiss

"Socratic Epistemology: Explorations of Knowledge-Seeking by Questioning" edited by Jaakko Hintikka

"The Socratic Paradox and Its Enemies" by Roslyn Weiss

"Socrates' Ancestor: An Essay on Architectural Beginnings" by Indra Kagis McEwen

Printed in Great Britain
by Amazon